Centers for Disease Control and Prevention

MMWR

Surveillance Summaries / Vol. 62 / No. 3

Morbidity and Mortality Weekly Report

July 19, 2013

Surveillance for Travel-Related Disease — GeoSentinel Surveillance System, United States, 1997–2011

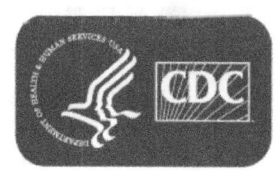

U.S. Department of Health and Human Services
Centers for Disease Control and Prevention

CONTENTS

Introduction 2

The GeoSentinel Surveillance System 3

Methods 6

Results 7

Discussion 13

Conclusion 14

Acknowledgments 14

References 15

Appendix A 16

Appendix B 18

Front cover photo: International travel connections between airports. Adapted from Hufnagel L, Brockmann D, Geisel T. Forecast and control of epidemics in a globalized world. Proceedings of the National Academy of Sciences 2004;101:15124–9. Copyright 2004, National Academy of Sciences, USA.

The *MMWR* series of publications is published by the Office of Surveillance, Epidemiology, and Laboratory Services, Centers for Disease Control and Prevention (CDC), U.S. Department of Health and Human Services, Atlanta, GA 30333.

Suggested Citation: Centers for Disease Control and Prevention. [Title]. MMWR 2013;62(No. SS-#):[inclusive page numbers].

Surveillance for Travel-Related Disease — GeoSentinel Surveillance System, United States, 1997–2011

Kira Harvey, MPH[1]
Douglas H. Esposito, MD[1]
Pauline Han, MA[1]
Phyllis Kozarsky, MD[1]
David O. Freedman, MD[2]
D. Adam Plier[2]
Mark J. Sotir, PhD[1]

[1]Division of Global Migration and Quarantine, National Center for Emerging and Zoonotic Infectious Disease, CDC
[2]Division of Infectious Diseases, Department of Medicine, University of Alabama at Birmingham, Birmingham, Alabama

Abstract

Problem/Condition: In 2012, the number of international tourist arrivals worldwide was projected to reach a new high of 1 billion arrivals, a 48% increase from 674 million arrivals in 2000. International travel also is increasing among U.S. residents. In 2009, U.S. residents made approximately 61 million trips outside the country, a 5% increase from 1999. Travel-related morbidity can occur during or after travel. Worldwide, 8% of travelers from industrialized to developing countries report becoming ill enough to seek health care during or after travel. Travelers have contributed to the global spread of infectious diseases, including novel and emerging pathogens. Therefore, surveillance of travel-related morbidity is an essential component of global public health surveillance and will be of greater importance as international travel increases worldwide.

Reporting Period: September 1997–December 2011.

Description of System: GeoSentinel is a clinic-based global surveillance system that tracks infectious diseases and other adverse health outcomes in returned travelers, foreign visitors, and immigrants. GeoSentinel comprises 54 travel/tropical medicine clinics worldwide that electronically submit demographic, travel, and clinical diagnosis data for all patients evaluated for an illness or other health condition that is presumed to be related to international travel. Clinical information is collected by physicians with expertise or experience in travel/tropical medicine. Data collected at all sites are entered electronically into a database, which is housed at and maintained by CDC. The GeoSentinel network membership program comprises 235 additional clinics in 40 countries on six continents. Although these network members do not report surveillance data systematically, they can report unusual or concerning diagnoses in travelers and might be asked to perform enhanced surveillance in response to specific health events or concerns.

Results: During September 1997–December 2011, data were collected on 141,789 patients with confirmed or probable travel-related diagnoses. Of these, 23,006 (16%) patients were evaluated in the United States, 10,032 (44%) of whom were evaluated after returning from travel outside of the United States (i.e., after-travel patients). Of the 10,032 after-travel patients, 4,977 (50%) were female, 4,856 (48%) were male, and 199 (2%) did not report sex; the median age was 34 years. Most were evaluated in outpatient settings (84%), were born in the United States (76%), and reported current U.S. residence (99%). The most common reasons for travel were tourism (38%), missionary/volunteer/research/aid work (24%), visiting friends and relatives (17%), and business (15%). The most common regions of exposure were Sub-Saharan Africa (23%), Central America (15%), and South America (12%). Fewer than half (44%) reported having had a pretravel visit with a health-care provider.

Of the 13,059 diagnoses among the 10,032 after-travel patients, the most common diagnoses were acute unspecified diarrhea (8%), acute bacterial diarrhea (5%), postinfectious irritable bowel syndrome (5%), giardiasis (3%), and chronic unknown diarrhea (3%). The most common diagnostic groupings were acute diarrhea (22%), nondiarrheal gastrointestinal (15%), febrile/systemic illness (14%), and dermatologic (12%). Among 1,802 patients with febrile/systemic illness diagnoses, the most common diagnosis was *Plasmodium falciparum* malaria (19%).

The rapid communication component of the GeoSentinel network has allowed prompt responses to important health events affecting travelers; during 2010 and 2011, the notification capability of the GeoSentinel network was used in the identification and public health response to East African trypanosomiasis in Eastern Zambia and North Central Zimbabwe, *P. vivax* malaria in Greece, and muscular sarcocystosis on Tioman Island, Malaysia.

Corresponding author: Kira Harvey, Division of Global Migration and Quarantine, National Center for Emerging and Zoonotic Infectious Disease, CDC. Telephone: 404-639-7717; E-mail: jii3@cdc.gov.

Interpretation: The GeoSentinel Global Surveillance System is the largest repository of provider-based data on travel-related illness. Among ill travelers evaluated in U.S. GeoSentinel sites after returning from international travel, gastrointestinal diagnoses were most frequent, suggesting that U.S. travelers might be exposed to unsafe food and water while traveling internationally. The most common febrile/systemic diagnosis was *P. falciparum* malaria, suggesting that some U.S. travelers to malarial areas are not receiving or using proper malaria chemoprophylaxis or mosquito-bite avoidance measures. The finding that fewer than half of all patients reported having made a pretravel visit with a health-care provider indicates that a substantial portion of U.S. travelers might not be following CDC travelers' health recommendations for international travel.

Public Health Action: GeoSentinel surveillance data have helped researchers define an evidence base for travel medicine that has informed travelers' health guidelines and the medical evaluation of ill international travelers. These data suggest that persons traveling internationally from the United States to developing countries remain at risk for illness. Health-care providers should help prepare travelers properly for safe travel and provide destination-specific medical evaluation of returning ill travelers. Training for health-care providers should focus on preventing and treating a variety of travel-related conditions, particularly traveler's diarrhea and malaria.

Introduction

Since the advent of modern commercial aviation in the 1950s, international civilian travel has increased steadily to record levels (*1*). In 2012, the number of international tourist arrivals worldwide was projected to reach a new high of 1 billion arrivals, a 48% increase from 674 million arrivals in 2000. Tourist destinations also have become increasingly diverse, with the proportion of international tourist arrivals in countries with emerging and developing economies increasing from 31% in 1990 to 47% in 2010. Tourism comprises approximately 5% of the total worldwide gross domestic product, and its contribution to many emerging economies is likely to be substantially higher (*1*).

International travel also is increasing among U.S. residents. In 2009, U.S. residents made 61 million overnight trips outside the country, representing a 5% increase from 1999 (*2*). This increase reflects not only traditional tourism but also travel for other purposes. For example, 14% of U.S. students pursuing a bachelor's degree study abroad at least once, and, for the 2010–2011 school year, 46% of these students studied in places outside Europe (*3*). In 2011, of 27,023,000 U.S. residents traveling overseas, 35% listed visiting friends and/ or family as their main purpose of travel (*4*). This includes immigrants and their children who return to their country of origin to visit friends and relatives (VFR travelers). U.S. residents also devote considerable resources to international travel and collectively spent $79.1 billion on international tourism in 2011. This expenditure represented 7.7% of the world's international tourism market, making the United States second only to Germany in terms of the international tourism market share (*1*).

International travelers can experience travel-related morbidity during and after travel. Of the approximately 50 million persons who travel from industrialized countries to developing countries each year, 8% report becoming ill enough to seek health care either during or after travel (*5,6*). Many other travelers also experience health problems that often go unreported (*6,7*). First- and second-generation immigrant VFR travelers are thought to experience a greater burden of travel-related disease than other types of travelers (*8,9*).

Travelers can contribute to the global spread of infectious diseases, including novel and emerging pathogens. In 2003, during the initial phase of the global epidemic of Severe Acute Respiratory Syndrome (SARS), an infected professor from southern China traveled to a major international hotel in Hong Kong, where he infected others. Persons infected with SARS subsequently traveled to other countries, leading to rapid worldwide spread of the disease (*10*). More recently, international travelers infected with novel H1N1 influenza played a major role in the rapid global spread of the virus (*11*). Travelers also have carried pathogens to areas of the world where these pathogens were rare or had been eliminated. Recent outbreaks of vaccine-preventable diseases such as measles (*12*) and mumps (*13*) in the United States have been traced to contact with persons who had traveled to locations where vaccination was less prevalent. In addition, travel and migration have contributed to recent introduction or reintroduction of vectorborne diseases in places that had been free from these diseases, such as locally acquired dengue in Florida (*14*) and malaria in Greece (*15*) and in Great Exuma Island in the Caribbean (*16*).

Description and evaluation of the patterns of disease among persons traveling internationally can provide information that might help prevent, treat, and control disease among international travelers and help prevent the global spread of pathogens. The timely detection of diseases in this population can alert the public health and medical communities to disease outbreaks before they spread to or become apparent in the general population.

The GeoSentinel Surveillance System (GeoSentinel) was established in 1995 to perform provider-based monitoring of travel-related morbidity among persons traveling internationally. The goals of GeoSentinel are to 1) improve the understanding of morbidity and disease acquisition among international travelers, and immigrants; 2) expand the evidence-base that guides pretravel health recommendations and the evaluation and medical management of the ill traveler; 3) enhance the detection of important health events occurring among this mobile population; and 4) create a communications network that allows rapid dissemination of important health information among medical practitioners, government bodies, and the public. GeoSentinel clinics worldwide collect demographic, travel, and clinical diagnosis surveillance data systematically from ill international travelers both during and after travel, using the best reference diagnostic methods available in their practice settings. Additional information on GeoSentinel and site locations is available at http://www.istm.org/Default.aspx.

This report describes the GeoSentinel surveillance system, documents its growth and evolution during 1995–2011, provides summary data from 22 U.S. sites that participated in the GeoSentinel network at any point during September 1997–December 2011 (the most recent year for which finalized data are available), and describes selected important health events in the worldwide GeoSentinel population during 2010–2011. The findings presented in this report will inform providers and public health agencies about the travel-related illnesses that are most commonly seen in returned travelers in the United States, which will help providers prepare travelers properly for safe international travel and also provide guidance for the evaluation and treatment of ill patients who seek medical care after travel.

The GeoSentinel Surveillance System

Establishment of GeoSentinel

In 1995, three members* of the International Society of Travel Medicine (ISTM) proposed a framework for GeoSentinel, a global provider-based surveillance system focused on patients evaluated at travel and tropical medicine clinics. Later that year, a working group of nine U.S.-based ISTM member travel clinics formally established GeoSentinel (17). At that time, approximately one third of ISTM clinics reported seeing more than 100 post-travel patients per year, and no systems were in place to compile patient data from these geographically dispersed small clinics (18). GeoSentinel was established to fill the need for a collaborative clinic-based global surveillance system designed to collect limited de-identified demographic, travel, and clinical data from returned international travelers, immigrants, and foreign visitors who visit clinics for evaluation of illnesses suspected to be related to travel (17).

These data, which can link place of acquisition of illness to time of exposure, can be used both to monitor disease burden and distribution and to detect the emergence of new human infections or new patterns of disease occurrence or transmission. In addition, by linking travel medicine clinics around the world, GeoSentinel can facilitate rapid communication of important information among medical practitioners, governmental bodies, and the public (17). By 1996, GeoSentinel had become organized as a cooperative effort between ISTM and CDC, and systematic data collection began in 1997.

GeoSentinel Sites

GeoSentinel sites are specialized travel/tropical medicine units; the GeoSentinel site director and a majority of contributing physicians have documented training and expertise in travel/tropical medicine and/or significant experience in the care of patients with travel-related or tropical diseases. Most sites are located within academic health centers (19). GeoSentinel sites are asked to submit completed reporting forms (Appendix A) for all patients evaluated for an illness or other health condition that is presumed to be travel-related.

After its inception, the number of sites in GeoSentinel increased steadily from the initial nine U.S. sites, with several European clinics being added during the first 2 years after data collection began. By 1999, GeoSentinel comprised an international network of 24 travel/tropical medicine clinics, 14 (58%) of which were located in the United States. During 2004–2005, in response to the increased concern for potential emerging diseases following the SARS epidemic, GeoSentinel received supplemental CDC funding to establish additional sites in Asia and elsewhere. These sites are known to treat a substantial number of travelers and expatriates who become ill and seek care while traveling. As of December 2011, the GeoSentinel Global Surveillance System comprised 54 member travel/tropical medicine clinics in 24 countries on six continents (Figure 1), including 17 (31%) sites in the United States.

* David O. Freedman, MD, University of Alabama at Birmingham; Phyllis Kozarsky, MD, Emory University, CDC; Martin Cetron, MD, CDC.

FIGURE 1. Locations of GeoSentinel surveillance sites* and network members†

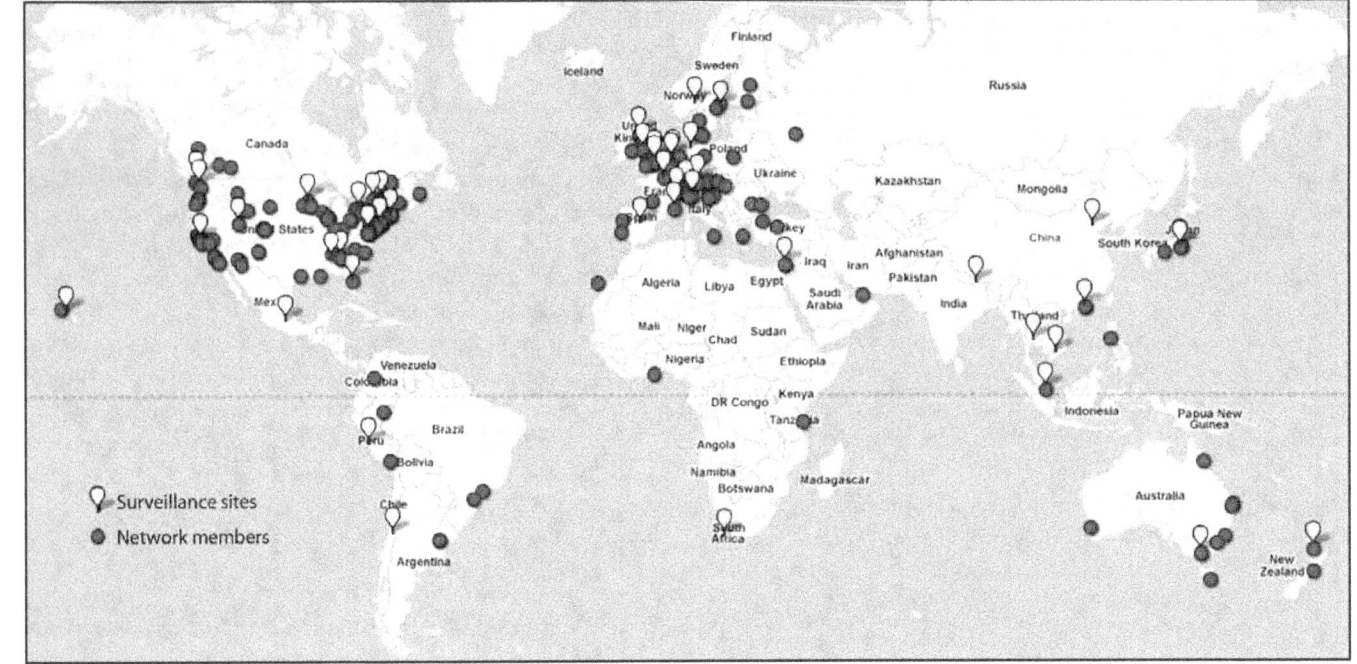

* N = 54.
† N = 235.

Network Members

In October 2001, the GeoSentinel Network expanded to include additional travel/tropical medicine providers who do not enter data from patient records into the GeoSentinel database. However, Network members can report noteworthy diagnoses in travelers and, along with the GeoSentinel clinic sites, might be asked to perform enhanced surveillance in response to important health events or concerns.

Network members also receive electronic mail from GeoSentinel, individual sites, and other Network members alerting them to unusual or noteworthy health events among travelers. Such alerts allow rapid linkage of and communication among a substantial number of clinics and health authorities around the world. This rapid communication infrastructure enables timely outbreak identification and response. As of April 2011, a total of 235 clinics in 40 countries on six continents were members of the GeoSentinel Network (Figure 1).

Variables and Definitions

GeoSentinel is limited to data concerning patients evaluated by medical providers at GeoSentinel clinics. Travelers must have crossed an international border within 10 years of clinic visit and have sought medical care for a presumed travel-related illness. Data from patients evaluated for other reasons within that 10-year timeframe and ultimately determined to have a travel-related illness also can be included. For each patient, GeoSentinel uses a form to collect 28 data elements pertaining to patient demographic information, travel history, presenting symptoms, and clinical diagnoses (Appendix A). The following definitions of variables are used:

Reason for travel: The main reason for travel related to the current illness; limited to a single designation (Box 1).

Expatriate: A person living in a destination country with a permanent residence and address and using mostly the infrastructure used by local residents, independent of travel duration.

Patient type: This includes classifications regarding whether the patient was evaluated in person, and whether that patient was an inpatient or an outpatient.

- *Inpatient:* The patient was seen at the reporting GeoSentinel site as an inpatient.
- *Outpatient:* The patient was seen at the reporting GeoSentinel site as an outpatient.
- *Tele-consult in-patient:* The patient's record was obtained after a doctor at the reporting GeoSentinel site provided a telephonic consultation regarding an inpatient at a different location.

BOX 1. Reason for travel (case definitions) as listed on questionnaire — GeoSentinel Surveillance Network

- **Tourism:** includes all travel for tourism or leisure. Also includes travel that may involve visits to friends and relatives overseas if the traveler is not a first- or second-generation immigrant returning to his/her country of origin.
- **Business:** includes all travel for business or occupational purposes.
- **Missionary/volunteer/researcher/aid worker:** includes all travel for volunteer, missionary work, relief work, or research.
- **Student:** includes all travel for study in a recognized educational institution or travel as part of a group trip under the sponsorship of a recognized educational institution, with the primary purpose of study or non-research educational activity. This category is not used for individuals traveling for other reasons who happen to be students.
- **Medical tourism:** includes all travel when entry into a country other than the patient's country of residence was for the primary purpose of seeking either emergency or elective medical care for conditions that existed prior to travel.
- **Immigration:** includes all travelers whose only relevant international travel is the primary immigration trip to the country of the reporting site. This applies to all immigrants and refugees regardless of legal status.
- **Visiting friends or relatives:** includes all first- or second-generation immigrants, originally from a low- or middle-income country now living in a high-income country, visiting friends or relatives in the patient's family's country of origin.
- **Military:** includes all travel for formal military deployment by a member of the military under field conditions and using accommodations shared with other members of the military. Does not include travel during leave.

- *Tele-consult outpatient:* The patient's record was obtained after a doctor at the recording GeoSentinel site provided a telephonic consultation regarding an outpatient at a different location.

Clinical setting: The timing of the clinic visit in relation to travel.
- *During travel:* The clinic visit occurred before the trip ended. Includes expatriates evaluated in the country of their expatriation for illnesses that most likely were acquired in that country or for which the country of exposure could not be ascertained.
- *After travel:* The clinic visit occurred after the trip ended. Includes expatriates with illnesses that most likely were acquired outside the country of their expatriation.
- *Immigration-only travel:* The clinic visit occurred after the primary immigration trip to the country of the reporting site, and the diagnosis is for an illness most likely acquired before immigration.

Travel-related: Designates the relation of the main diagnosis to the patient's travel.
- *Travel-related:* Used when the illness under evaluation, initially suspected to be travel-related, was determined to have been acquired during the patient's travel.
- *Not travel-related:* Used when the illness under evaluation, initially suspected to be travel related, was determined to have been acquired before departure from or after returning to the home country.
- *Not ascertainable:* Used when the illness under evaluation, initially suspected to be travel related, was equally likely to have been acquired during the patient's travel or before departing from or after returning to the residence country.

Diagnosis and diagnosis type: Medical providers or coders choose from approximately 500 widely varied diagnoses determined by CDC-ISTM consensus, each of which is classified as either etiologic or syndromic. A write-in option is available for diagnoses not included on the list. The diagnosis list has evolved to reflect the changing needs of the network (Appendix B) (20).
- *Etiologic:* This diagnosis type reflects specific disease etiologies (e.g., malaria or *Plasmodium falciparum*). The "diagnosis status" of etiologic diagnoses might be confirmed, probable, or suspect (see Diagnosis status).
- *Syndromic:* This diagnosis type reflects symptom- or syndrome-based etiologies (e.g., gastroenteritis) when a more specific etiology is not known or could not be determined as a result of use of empiric therapy, self-limited disease, or inability to justify additional diagnostic tests beyond standard clinical practice. The "diagnosis status" of all syndromic diagnoses is "confirmed" (see Diagnosis status).

Diagnosis status: The strength of the diagnosis is categorized in one of three ways:

- *Confirmed:* Diagnosis has been made by an indisputable clinical finding or diagnostic test. "Syndromic" diagnoses are always considered to be "confirmed."
- *Probable:* Diagnosis is supported by evidence strong enough to establish presumption but not proof.
- *Suspect:* Diagnosis warrants consideration on the basis of a clinical finding or laboratory result.

Syndrome/System groupings of diagnoses: All GeoSentinel diagnoses are categorized into groups (Box 2).

Main presenting symptom: The predefined grouping is used to categorize the patient's main presenting symptom(s). As many symptom groups as are required can be coded for each patient. Patients without symptoms can be included in one of the following two groupings.

- *Screening:* The patient underwent risk-based screening for a travel-related disease.
- *Abnormal laboratory test:* The patient was referred to the GeoSentinel site because an abnormal result was found on a laboratory test that was performed elsewhere.

BOX 2. Syndrome/system groupings for available GeoSentinel diagnoses — GeoSentinel Surveillance Network

- Acute diarrhea
- Adverse event to medication or vaccination
- Cardiovascular
- Chronic disease
- Chronic diarrhea
- Dermatologic
- Febrile/systemic illness
- Genitourinary and sexually transmitted infections
- Injury and musculoskeletal
- Tissue parasites
- Neurologic
- Nonspecific symptoms or findings
- Obstetric/gynecologic
- Ophthalmologic
- Oral and dental
- Other gastrointestinal
- Psychological
- Respiratory

Data Collection

Initially, following the development of a standard data collection form in 1997, GeoSentinel used a paper-based data collection system. Sites completed a form for each patient with an illness presumed to be travel-related. Completed forms were then sent to CDC for the information to be entered into the database.

In April 2001, sites began using a web-based data submission system as they gained access to the requisite technology. The web-based data submission system contains the same fields as the paper data collection forms. In 2002, all sites were given the option of submitting data using the web-based data submission system. All sites were formally offered access to the web-based data submission system in June 2002. By September 2002, the web-based data submission system was being used by 10 of 32 sites. Also beginning in 2002, stepwise improvements to the data entry website were made to reduce the number of data entry errors and expand data functionality (Box 3).

In May 2007, a second-generation web-based data entry application was introduced. By this time, all 32 GeoSentinel sites were providing patient data via the Internet. The second-generation data-entry application featured a complete redesign of both the data entry application and the database. An improved user interface included internal validation, which prevented entry of contradictory data.

Methods

This report summarizes data from patients with at least one final travel-related diagnosis who were evaluated at the 22 current and past GeoSentinel sites located in the United States during September 1997–December 2011. These 22 sites did not necessarily submit data every year of the reporting period. Patients must have been evaluated within 10 years of returning from a trip outside of the United States. The final travel-related diagnosis must have been classified as probable or confirmed. Only patients who were evaluated in a clinical setting (i.e., the timing of clinic visit in relation to travel) that was classified as after-travel were included in this analysis. Patients evaluated in a clinical setting classified as during travel or immigration only were excluded from the analysis. No restriction was placed on resident status (i.e., data from both U.S. and non-U.S. resident patients were included).

Analysis

This report presents the results of a descriptive analysis from data collected at the 22 current and past GeoSentinel sites located in the United States. No statistical tests of significance were performed. Frequencies were calculated for the following after-travel patient characteristics: sex, age group (<19, 19–34, 35–49, 50–64, and ≥65 years), patient type (i.e., inpatient or outpatient status), birth country (United States versus non–United States), country of residence (United States versus

BOX 3. Changes to the GeoSentinel data entry application over time — GeoSentinel Surveillance Network, 1997–2011

January 1997
- GeoSentinel began collecting data using standard paper forms.

April 2001
- A select number of sites began beta-testing a web-based data submission system.

June 2002
- All sites were given the option of submitting data using the web-based system.

September 2002
- 10 of 32 sites were using web-based data entry. New features added included: 1) searchable country look-up list, and 2) autofill option for "Country of Residence/Country of Citizenship/Country of Residence Before Age 10."

June 2004
- The data entry system began to allow free-text diagnosis information.

June 2005
- Review of commonly used free-text diagnoses in the database led to the creation of new diagnosis codes and revision of existing diagnosis codes.

September 2005
- "Medical tourism" was added as a "Reason for Travel" and "Primary Complaint" was changed to "Main Presenting Symptom."

May 2007
- Second-generation web-based data entry was introduced. New features added included: 1) data entry process was streamlined, 2) separate checkboxes for immigrants and expatriates were created, and 3) the online "Help" system was expanded.

September 2007
- All "Syndromic" diagnoses were characterized as "Confirmed" diagnosis status.
- "Etiologic" diagnoses could not be characterized as "etiology unknown."
- Maximum number of possible exposure countries permitted decreased from three to two.
- "Immigrant" was defined as a person who has emigrated from country of birth and does not apply to persons who have emigrated within Western Europe, between the United States and Canada, or between Australia and New Zealand.

February 2010
- An algorithm was added to automatically calculate region of exposure.

May 2011
- The following data fields became mandatory for each record: "Travel Related," "Expatriate," and "Pretravel Encounter."

non–United States), reason for travel (Box 1) or expatriate status, pretravel encounter, and region of exposure. Region of exposure was calculated on the basis of the most likely country or countries of exposure (limited to two countries). If two countries in different regions were listed as country of exposure, then the region of exposure was not listed. Frequencies of final travel-related diagnoses and syndrome/system groupings of diagnoses also were determined (Appendix B). Patients could have one or more than one final travel-related diagnosis. For the top three regions of travel, the top two diagnoses by region also were determined. The region of exposure for current illness was assigned by using modified UNICEF groupings (Figure 2). For all frequency calculations, records with unknown or missing data were included in each denominator. Analyses were conducted by using SAS version 9.3 (SAS Institute, Inc., Cary, North Carolina).

Selected Worldwide Health Event Notifications

To illustrate the notification capability of the GeoSentinel Network, three examples of important health events occurring during 2010 and 2011 are described. These health events were not limited to U.S. sites and included patients seen elsewhere in the global network.

Results

During September 1997–December 2011, a total of 164,378 patients were evaluated at GeoSentinel sites worldwide (U.S. and non-U.S.) and included in the GeoSentinel Surveillance System's database. Of these, 141,789 (86%) received at least one final confirmed or probable travel-related diagnosis; 23,006

FIGURE 2. Geographic region* of exposure for after-travel patients — GeoSentinel Surveillance System, worldwide, 2011

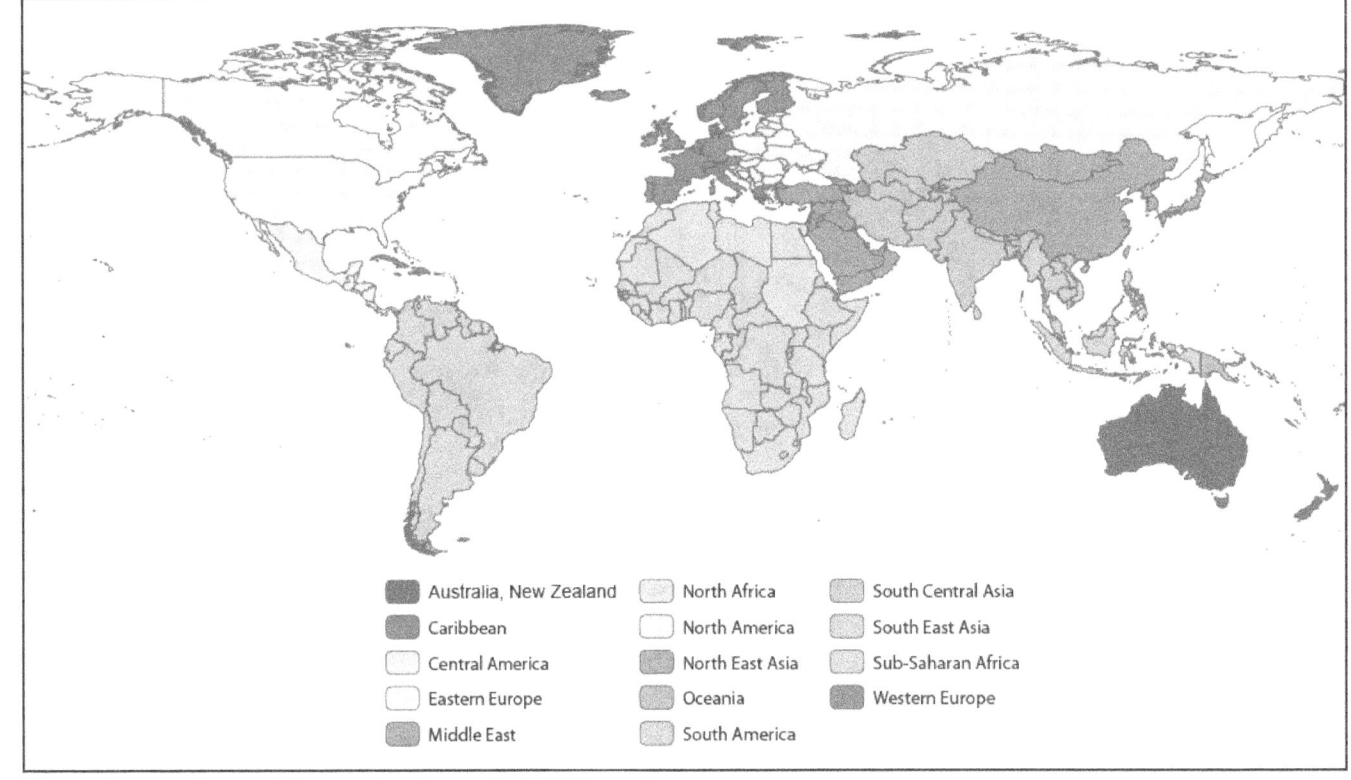

* Region of exposure for current illness was based on modified UNICEF groupings.

(16%) were reported from 22 current and past GeoSentinel sites in the United States. Included in this analysis were 10,032 after-travel patients (Figure 3), with 13,059 confirmed or probable final diagnoses (1.3 diagnoses per patient).

During September 1997–December 2011, the number of patients evaluated at U.S. GeoSentinel sites and included in the GeoSentinel database per year increased, as has the proportion of all patients evaluated after travel (Figure 4). During 1998, a total of 971 patients were seen at U.S. GeoSentinel sites and included in the GeoSentinel database, 333 (34%) of whom were patients evaluated after travel. In 2011, a total of 2,344 patients were evaluated at U.S. GeoSentinel sites and included in the GeoSentinel database, 1,199 (51%) of whom were patients evaluated after travel.

After-Travel Patients from U.S. GeoSentinel Sites

Of the 10,032 after-travel patients who were evaluated at U.S. GeoSentinel sites during September 1997–December 2011 and who received a diagnosis, a total of 4,977 (50%) were female and 4,856 number (48%) were male; sex was not reported for 199 (2%) patients. The median age was 34 years.

By age group, 735 (7%) were aged <19 years, 4,398 (44%) were aged 19–34 years, 2,343 (23%) were aged 35–49 years, 1,850 (18%) were aged 50–64 years, and 622 (6%) were aged ≥65 years (Table 1). Most (84%) patients were evaluated in an outpatient setting. More than three fourths (76%) of patients were born in the United States, and nearly all (99%) were current U.S. residents.

The most common reason for travel among the after-travel patients who received a diagnosis was tourism (38%); other reasons for travel included being a missionary/volunteer/researcher/aid worker (24%), a VFR traveler (17%), a business person (15%), a student (6%), a member of the military (<1%), and a medical tourist (<1%). Approximately 12% of patients were expatriates. Fewer than half of all patients (44%) reported consulting a medical provider before traveling in preparation for their international trip.

The most common region of exposure was Sub-Saharan Africa (23%). Other common regions of exposure included Central America (15%), South America (12%), the Caribbean (9%), South Central Asia (8%), and South East Asia (7%). Less common regions of exposure included Western Europe (5%), North East Asia (3%), the Middle East (2%), North Africa (2%), Eastern Europe (1%), Oceania (1%), North

FIGURE 3. Flowchart of patients included in the GeoSentinel database — GeoSentinel Surveillance System, worldwide, 1997–2011

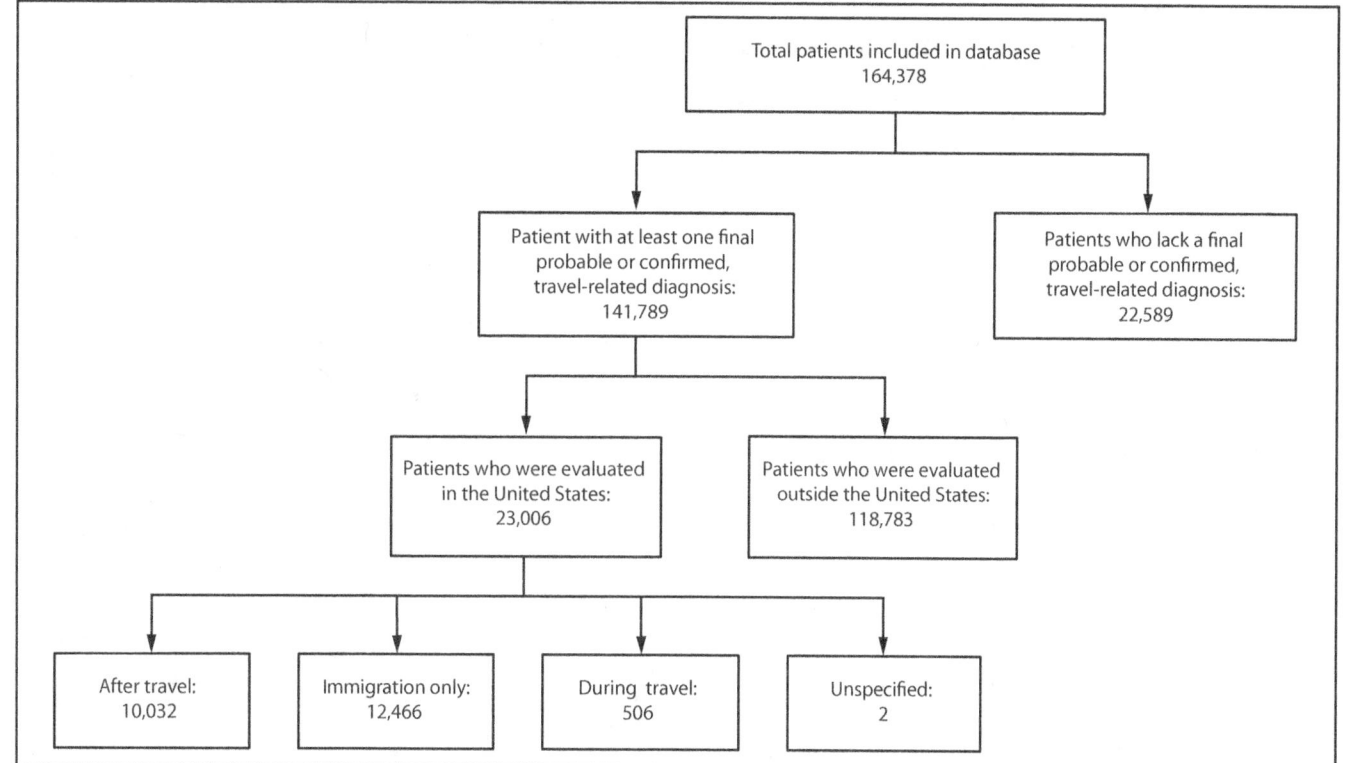

America (<1%), and Australia/New Zealand (<1%). Region of exposure could not be determined or was not reported for 11% of patients (Table 1).

Diagnoses

Of the 13,059 diagnoses included in analysis, the most common were acute unspecified diarrhea (8%), acute bacterial diarrhea (5%), postinfectious irritable bowel syndrome (5%), giardia (3%), chronic unknown diarrhea (3%), *P. falciparum* malaria (3%), viral syndrome without rash (2%), simple intestinal strongyloides (2%), blastocystis (2%), and upper respiratory tract infection (2%) (Table 2). Eighty-four percent of specific diagnoses fell into eight syndromic groupings: acute diarrhea (22%), other gastrointestinal (15%), febrile/systemic disease (14%), dermatologic (12%), chronic diarrhea (8%), respiratory (8%), and nonspecific signs and symptoms (5%) (Table 3).

Of the 2,811 diagnoses in the acute diarrhea grouping, 80% were accounted for by five diagnoses: acute unspecified diarrhea (36%), acute bacterial diarrhea (23%), giardia (13%), amoebas (4%), and campylobacter (4%). Of the 1,908 diagnoses in the other gastrointestinal grouping, five diagnoses comprised 48%: simple intestinal strongyloides (15%), blastocystis (15%), abdominal pain (6%), esophagitis (6%), and *Helicobacter*

pylori-positive gastritis (6%). Among the 1,100 diagnoses in the chronic diarrhea grouping, 95% were accounted for by five diagnoses: postinfectious irritable bowel syndrome (55%), chronic unknown diarrhea (32%), irritable bowel syndrome (4%), ulcerative colitis (3%), and postinfectious lactose intolerance (1%).

Of the 1,802 diagnoses in the febrile/systemic disease grouping, 59% were accounted for by five diagnoses: *P. falciparum* malaria (19%), viral syndrome without rash (17%), uncomplicated dengue (11%), unspecified febrile disease (<3 weeks) (8%), and Epstein-Barr virus (4%). In the respiratory grouping, 70% of 1,002 diagnoses were accounted for by five diagnoses: upper respiratory tract infection (27%), acute bronchitis (18%), acute sinusitis (11%), bacterial pneumonia (lobar) (8%), and asthma (6%). In the dermatologic grouping, 44% of 1,596 were accounted for by five diagnoses: insect bite/sting (15%), nonfebrile rash of unknown etiology (10%), fungal infection (superficial/cutaneous mycosis) (7%), cutaneous leishmaniasis (6%), and skin and soft tissue infection (6%). In the nonspecific symptoms grouping, 72% of 702 diagnoses were accounted for by eosinophilia (28%), fatigue for at least 1 month (nonfebrile) (18%), fatigue for <1 month (nonfebrile) (14%), anemia (8%), and weight loss (4%).

FIGURE 4. Number* of patients evaluated in the United States and included in the GeoSentinel database, by year and clinical setting — United States, 1997–2011

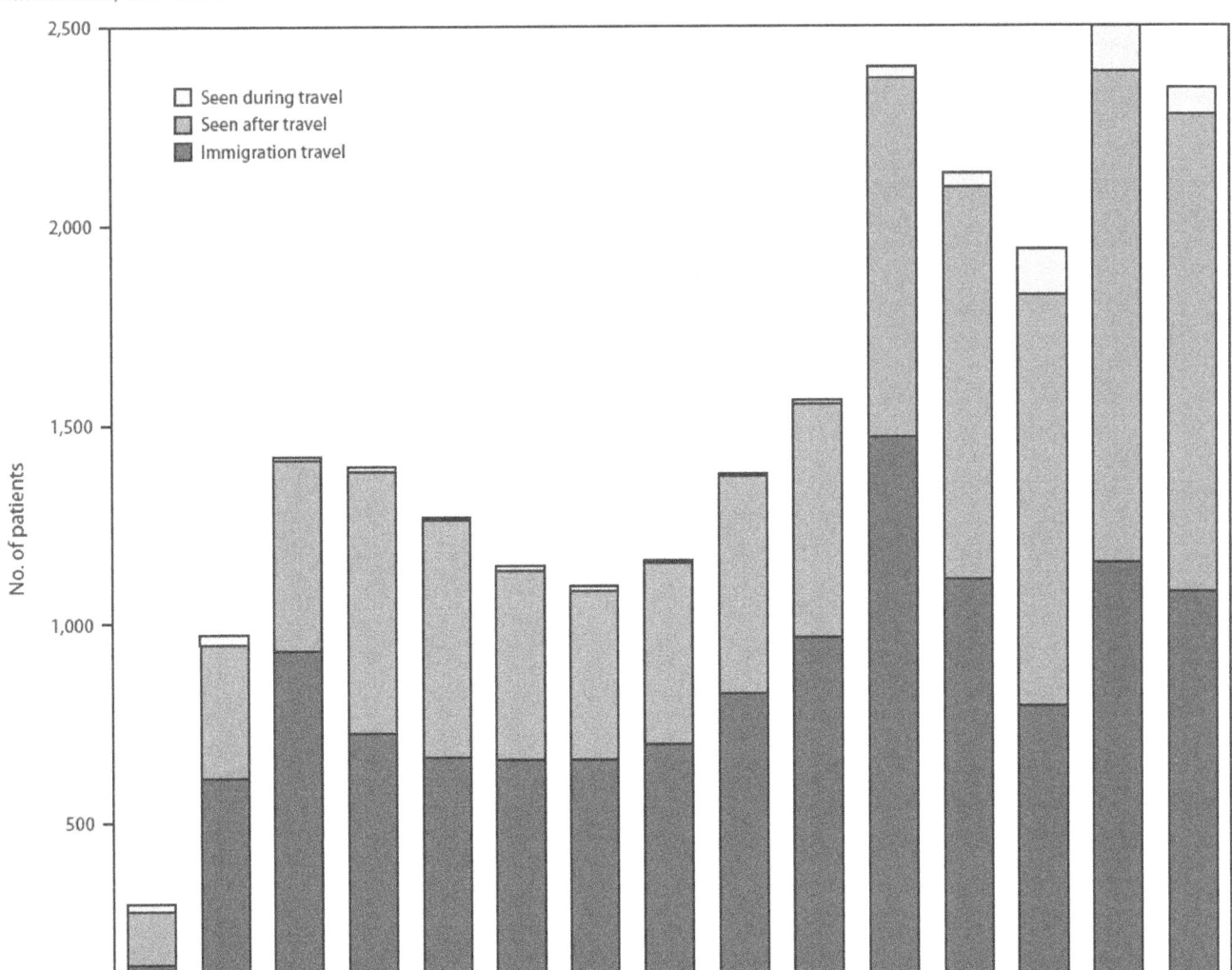

* N = 23,004. The 22 GeoSentinel sites did not all necessarily submit data in every year of the reporting period.

Of 3,069 diagnoses among patients exposed to their illnesses in Sub-Saharan Africa, the most frequent were *P. falciparum* malaria (10%) and acute unspecified diarrhea (6%). Over half (58%) of *P. falciparum* malaria diagnoses among patients exposed in Sub-Saharan Africa occurred among VFR travelers, and 6% of acute unspecified diarrhea diagnoses in this group occurred among VFR travelers. Of the 1,977 diagnoses among patients exposed in Central America, the most frequent were acute unspecified diarrhea (13%) and acute bacterial diarrhea (6%). Of the 1,562 diagnoses among patients exposed in South America, the most frequent were acute unspecified diarrhea (8%) and postinfectious irritable bowel syndrome (7%). Of the 1,186 diagnoses among patients exposed in the Caribbean, the most frequent were acute unspecified diarrhea (6%) and acute bacterial diarrhea (5%).

TABLE 1. Number* and percentage of travelers evaluated after travel at U.S. GeoSentinel Sites who received at least one confirmed or probable travel-related final diagnosis — GeoSentinel Surveillance System, United States, 1997–2011

Characteristic	No.	(%)
Sex		
Female	4,977	(50)
Male	4,856	(48)
Missing	199	(2)
Age group		
<19 yrs	735	(7)
19–34 yrs	4,398	(44)
35–49 yrs	2,343	(23)
50–64 yrs	1,850	(18)
≥65 yrs	622	(6)
Missing	84	(<1)
Patient type		
Outpatient	8,372	(84)
Inpatient	707	(7)
Teleconsult outpatient	439	(4)
Teleconsult inpatient	84	(<1)
Missing	430	(4)
Born/Residence in US		
Born in the United States	7,597	(76)
Residence in the United States	9,942	(99)
Reason for travel		
Tourism	3,799	(38)
Missionary/volunteer/researcher/aid worker	2,438	(24)
Visiting friends and relatives	1,661	(17)
Business	1,492	(15)
Student	582	(6)
Military	18	(<1)
Medical tourism	9	(<1)
Missing	33	(<1)
Expatriate	1,154	(12)
Pretravel encounter		
Yes	4,451	(44)
No	4,134	(41)
Unknown	887	(9)
Missing	560	(6)
Region of exposure		
Sub-Saharan Africa	2,276	(23)
Central America	1,550	(15)
South America	1,219	(12)
Caribbean	947	(9)
South Central Asia	774	(8)
South East Asia	696	(7)
Western Europe	453	(5)
North East Asia	321	(3)
Middle East	207	(2)
North Africa	179	(2)
Eastern Europe	144	(1)
Oceania	108	(1)
North America	42	(<1)
Australia/New Zealand	28	(<1)
Missing	1,088	(11)

* N = 10,032.

TABLE 2. Number* and percentage of confirmed and probable final diagnoses in travelers evaluated after travel at GeoSentinel sites — GeoSentinel Surveillance System, United States, 1997–2011

Diagnosis	No.	(%)
Diarrhea, acute unspecified	1,023	(8)
Diarrhea, acute bacterial	639	(5)
Irritable bowel syndrome, postinfectious	605	(5)
Giardiasis	376	(3)
Diarrhea, chronic unknown	351	(3)
Malaria, *P. falciparum*	350	(3)
Viral syndrome (no rash)	308	(2)
Strongyloides, simple intestinal	292	(2)
Blastocystis, specified	289	(2)
Upper respiratory tract infection	269	(2)

* N = 13,059.

Selected Health Event Notifications in GeoSentinel, 2010–2011

The GeoSentinel network is designed to allow rapid communication about important health events among travelers. This enhanced communication has allowed prompt outbreak response from CDC and other clinical and public health entities worldwide. Three recent important health events exemplify the notification capability of GeoSentinel.

Event 1: East African Trypanosomiasis in Eastern Zambia and North Central Zimbabwe

In late August 2010, a GeoSentinel site in the United States reported a male patient with *Trypanosoma brucei rhodesiense* (East African trypanosomiasis [EAT]). This patient was a hunter who had traveled recently to Zambia. The site later confirmed that less than 2 weeks prior to visiting a GeoSentinel site, the patient had traveled to a game reserve in the South Luangwa River Valley, where he was bitten by tsetse flies. This situation was unusual because no instances of EAT among international travelers to Zambia had been reported since 2000 (*21*), and the last reported occurrence of a U.S. traveler with EAT acquired in Zambia occurred in 1986 (*22*).

During October 21–November 21, 2010, three additional patients who were evaluated at three other GeoSentinel sites received a diagnosis of EAT. All three reported travel to the South Luangwa River Valley region in Zambia or the neighboring Mana Pools region in northern Zimbabwe. These patients and additional patients exposed in the same region but not identified through the GeoSentinel Network have been reported elsewhere (*23,24*).

On November 11, 2010, a GeoSentinel project director sent all sites and network members an alert describing the EAT occurrences and recommending that clinicians consider EAT

TABLE 3. Number* and percentage of diagnoses[†] within syndrome/system groupings in travelers observed after travel — GeoSentinel Surveillance System, United States, 1997–2011

Syndrome/System grouping Diagnosis	No.	(%)
Acute diarrhea	**2,811**	**(22)**
Diarrhea, acute unspecified	1,023	(36)
Diarrhea, acute bacterial	639	(23)
Giardiasis	376	(13)
Amebas, other (*Escherichia hartmani, E. nana, E. coli, E. polecki*)	122	(4)
Campylobacter	122	(4)
Gastrointestinal other	**1,908**	**(15)**
Strongyloides, simple intestinal	292	(15)
Blastocystis Sp.	289	(15)
Pain, abdominal	123	(6)
Esophagitis	114	(60
Gastritis, *Helicobacter pylori* positive	114	(6)
Febrile/Systemic illness	**1,802**	**(14)**
Plasmodium falciparum malaria	350	(19)
Viral syndrome (no rash)	308	(17)
Dengue, uncomplicated	200	(11)
Febrile illness unspecified (<3 weeks)	147	(8)
Epstein-Barr virus	79	(4)
Dermatologic	**1,596**	**(12)**
Insect bite/sting	237	(15)
Nonfebrile rash of unknown etiology	166	(10)
Fungal infection (superficial/cutaneous mycosis)	105	(7)
Cutaneous leishmaniasis	100	(6)
Skin and soft tissue infection	94	(6)
Chronic diarrhea	**1,100**	**(8)**
Irritable bowel syndrome, post-infectious	605	(55)
Chronic unknown diarrhea	351	(32)
Irritable bowel syndrome	44	(4)
Ulcerative colitis	31	(3)
Postinfectious lactose intolerance	15	(1)
Respiratory	**1,002**	**(8)**
Upper respiratory tract infection	879	(27)
Acute bronchitis	181	(18)
Acute sinusitis	107	(11)
Bacterial pneumonia (lobar)	79	(8)
Asthma	65	(6)
Nonspecific symptoms	**701**	**(5)**
Eosinophilia	199	(28)
Fatigue ≥1 month (nonfebrile)	128	(18)
Fatigue <1 month (nonfebrile)	98	(14)
Anemia	59	(8)
Weight loss	25	(4)
Chronic disease	294	(2)
Genitourinary/STDs	259	(2)
Psychological	238	(2)
Injury and musculoskeletal	217	(2)
Neurologic	223	(2)
Miscellaneous tissue parasites	211	(2)
Oral/Dental	131	(1)
Adverse events to medication or vaccination	98	(1)
Cardiovascular	80	(1)
Ob/Gyn	39	(<1)
Ophthalmologic	31	(<1)
Death	3	(<1)
Other	200	(2)
Lost to follow-up	115	(1)

Abbreviations: STDs = sexually transmitted diseases; ob/gyn = obstetric/gynecologic.
* N = 13,059.
[†] The five most common diagnoses are provided for the seven most common syndrome/system groupings.

as a diagnosis in travelers returning from Eastern Zambia and North Central Zimbabwe. In March 2012, CDC's Travelers' Health Branch posted a travel notice advising travelers to parts of East Africa to avoid tsetse fly bites and to watch for symptoms of EAT if they are bitten.

Event 2: *Plasmodium vivax* malaria in Greece

In August 2011, a GeoSentinel network member in Romania reported to a GeoSentinel Project Director about a patient with *Plasmodium vivax* malaria whose only recent travel was to the Skala and Elos regions of Greece (*25*). Although malaria was eradicated officially in Greece in 1974, subsequent instances of autochthonous (introduced) transmission of imported malaria to local residents in this region have been reported (*15*). Before this event, the most recent reported occurrences of malaria in travelers to Greece were in 2000 in a German couple with a history of travel to Kassandra, which is located in Chalkidiki (*26*). On August 19, 2011, a GeoSentinel project director alerted all GeoSentinel sites and network members of this event and asked them to be aware of these events when preparing travelers to and evaluating febrile travelers from the Skala and Elos regions of Greece. The Hellenic Centre for Disease Control and Prevention later published a report about 20 nontraveling Greeks who developed *P. vivax* malaria between May and September of 2011 (*27*). Recognition of this occurrence ultimately informed CDC malaria guidelines for travelers to Greece.

Event 3: Muscular sarcocystosis on Tioman Island, Malaysia

On October 25, 2011, a GeoSentinel site in Munich reported seven ill German travelers with fever, significant muscle pain, eosinophilia, and elevated serum creatinine phosphokinase. All seven travelers tested negative for both trichinosis and toxoplasmosis, and all had vacationed on islands off the east coast of peninsular Malaysia during the previous summer. A muscle biopsy from one of the patients revealed a single intracellular structure consistent with muscular sarcocystosis, a rarely reported disease caused by infection with *Sarcocystis* species. By October 27, 2011, as a result of a series of notifications to the GeoSentinel network, nine GeoSentinel sites and one non-GeoSentinel clinic in Europe, Asia, and North America had reported that 23 patients had been evaluated with similar symptoms; all had traveled to Tioman Island, Malaysia. On October 31, 2011, these patients were reported on ProMED-mail (*28*). By November 30, 2011, a total of 32 patients with suspected sarcocystosis had been reported to GeoSentinel (*29*).

On November 17, 2011, with assistance from EuroTravNet[†] and CDC and with support from the European Centre for Disease Prevention and Control and TropNet,[§] GeoSentinel launched an investigation to describe the demographic, travel, and clinical characteristics of these patients and to identify a possible common source of exposure on Tioman Island. On December 6, 2011, CDC's Travelers' Health Branch posted an outbreak notice for sarcocystosis in Malaysia, which included recommendations for safe food and water consumption and proper hygiene. On January 20, 2012, CDC published preliminary information on the outbreak (29). GeoSentinel sites continue to be alert to identify sarcocystis in patients returning from Malaysia.

Discussion

GeoSentinel is a clinic-based global surveillance system that tracks infectious diseases and other adverse health outcomes in returned travelers, foreign visitors, and immigrants. This system supplements traditional laboratory-based surveillance by focusing on the collection of data from a specific mobile population and linking data from clinics around the world. The collected data reflect a broad spectrum of etiologic and syndromic tropical and travel-related diseases, and documents the time and place of disease acquisition. Before the establishment of GeoSentinel, no system was in place to compile disease data on this population. GeoSentinel monitors disease among international travelers and can detect emergence of novel or re-emergent pathogens or changing patterns of transmission or acquisition of known diseases. GeoSentinel has grown substantially over time to comprise 54 member travel/ tropical medicine clinics in 24 countries on six continents, with 2,344 records entered from U.S. sites in 2011.

Data collected by GeoSentinel have been used to inform recommendations for travelers and for health-care providers involved in travel medicine. *CDC Health Information for International Travel* (the Yellow Book) includes numerous published reports from GeoSentinel (30). GeoSentinel also has detected unusual and important health events among travelers and alerted the public health and medical communities worldwide about these occurrences. The recent outbreak of *Sarcocystis*-like illness in travelers returning from Tioman Island is an example of GeoSentinel sites detecting an outbreak that had not been detected by any other surveillance system. Sarcocystosis is not a reportable disease in any country; this

outbreak was detected because of the efficient communication among GeoSentinel sites.

GeoSentinel has the capacity to identify and respond rapidly to aberrations in geographic patterns of illness among travelers, which is particularly important if these travelers originate from multiple nations or regions. GeoSentinel has played a role in identifying outbreaks in the past, including an outbreak of leptospirosis among travelers to Borneo, Malaysia, in 2000 (31). The identification by GeoSentinel of a Romanian traveler who acquired *P. vivax* malaria in Greece contributed to the investigation of a possible resurgence of malaria transmission there and ultimately informed CDC malaria prophylaxis guidelines for U.S. travelers to the affected region (27,28). The identification by GeoSentinel of incidents of EAT among tourists to Zambia and the adjacent Mana Pools region of Zimbabwe demonstrates that *Trypanosoma brucei rhodesiense* continues to be a threat to the health of travelers to this region. This is especially important because no cases had been reported among travelers during the preceding decade (24). These three important health events demonstrate that GeoSentinel is an effective communications network for clinical and public health information.

Data from U.S. GeoSentinel sites demonstrate that the majority of ill returned travelers in the GeoSentinel database evaluated at U.S. sites are encountered as outpatients and are aged 19–64 years; were traveling for tourism, business, or volunteer purposes; and were returning from Sub-Saharan Africa, Central America, or South America. In comparison with returned travelers evaluated at GeoSentinel sites worldwide during 1999–2011 (19,20), travelers evaluated at GeoSentinel sites in the United States during 1997–2011 (as described in this report) were exposed to their illnesses more frequently in Central America or South America and less frequently in South Central Asia or Southeast Asia. This likely reflects different travel patterns among U.S. travelers in comparison with travelers from Europe.

Among patients presenting to U.S. GeoSentinel sites, gastrointestinal diagnoses were recorded most frequently of all syndromic groupings. Acute unspecified diarrhea was among the top two diagnoses for each of the top four regions of exposure (Sub-Saharan Africa, South America, Central America, and Caribbean). These findings suggest that travelers might be exposed regularly to unsafe food or water during international trips. A substantial proportion of these diagnoses, including approximately half of both acute and chronic diarrhea diagnoses, were not attributed to any specific etiology. This reflects the fact that the specialized tests required for diagnosis of some of the most common causes of acute travelers' diarrhea, such as enterotoxigenic *E. coli* (ETEC),

---

[†] Additional information about EuroTravNet is available at http://www.istm. org/eurotravnet/main.html.

[§] Additional information about TropNet is available at http://www.tropnet.net.

are not used routinely in clinical practice (*19*). Although there are commonalities in diseases encountered by region of travel, the findings also demonstrate the importance of the use of GeoSentinel data to identify specific differences that vary by region of travel and by specific groups of travelers.

The most frequent diagnosis among the febrile/systemic grouping, as well as the most frequent diagnosis among patients exposed in Sub-Saharan Africa, was *P. falciparum* malaria. Approximately half of patients who contracted *P. falciparum* malaria in Sub-Saharan Africa were VFR travelers. Case-based malaria surveillance in the United States also has demonstrated that most *P. falciparum* cases occur among VFR travelers (*32*). VFR travelers experience increased burden of travel-related diseases, including malaria (*33*). Because these data indicate that malaria in U.S. travelers to malaria-endemic areas remains a concern, continuing to promote proper malaria chemoprophylaxis and mosquito bite avoidance to all travelers to malaria-endemic regions of the world should remain a priority. In addition, persons returning from these areas who develop a febrile illness should seek health care immediately, and practitioners should consider malaria as a possible cause for the illness.

CDC recommends that international travelers seek a pretravel medical consultation 4–6 weeks before traveling (*34*). However, the findings of this report indicate that fewer than half of ill returned travelers evaluated at U.S. GeoSentinel clinics during 1997–2011 reported having had a pretravel encounter with a health-care provider. Many of these travelers visited countries where diseases with limited or no presence in the United States are endemic. Such diseases include malaria, dengue, typhoid, and viral hepatitis. These and other potentially preventable diseases pose health risks to international travelers. Therefore, future efforts should seek to increase the number of travelers who seek pretravel medical consultation in accordance with the CDC recommendation. In addition, health-care providers who see travelers before travel should consider country- and region-specific vaccination, prophylaxis, and disease avoidance recommendations when presented with a traveler's itinerary. Increased use of pretravel consultations, along with improved education for health-care professionals, could result in a decrease in the burden of travel-related disease among U.S. international travelers.

Limitations

The data collected by GeoSentinel are subject to at least four limitations. First, because the findings are limited to travelers who visit participating GeoSentinel Sites, the data are not necessarily representative of all international travelers. As a result, the severity and frequency of illness among returned travelers might be underestimated. Second, because of the lack of denominator data, GeoSentinel data cannot be used to calculate travel-related disease rates or risks. Third, despite the use of standard diagnosis codes, data coding and entry practices might vary by site and over time. Finally, because the GeoSentinel data system has undergone numerous changes (Box 3) and the number of GeoSentinel sites has changed, direct comparisons over time might not be valid.

Conclusion

GeoSentinel is a global, clinic-based surveillance system that collects demographic, travel, and clinical diagnosis surveillance data from ill international travelers during and after travel. The system aims to improve understanding of morbidity in international travelers, inform health recommendations for travelers, and detect important health events among international travelers. Since 1999, GeoSentinel data have been used extensively to characterize travel-related illness (*17,19,20*) such as malaria (*35*) and dengue (*36*). Data from GeoSentinel sites have also been used to link particular travel destinations with rare or geographically unusual diseases among returned travelers (*23–25,29*). Future efforts to improve GeoSentinel's ability to characterize travel-related illness could include systematic collection of more detailed information from patients.

The findings in this report suggest that travelers from the United States to developing countries remain at risk for travel-related illness. To mitigate this risk, health-care providers should provide evidence-based advice to travelers before travel, as well as destination-specific medical evaluation to ill travelers after travel. Physicians who evaluate travelers before or after travel should be trained on prevention and treatment of a variety of travel-related conditions, with special attention paid to traveler's diarrhea and malaria.

Acknowledgments

The following members of the GeoSentinel Surveillance Network contributed data from U.S. sites: DeVon C. Hale, MD, Rahul Anand, MD, Stephanie S. Gelman, MD, University of Utah, Salt Lake City, Utah; Bradley A. Connor, MD, Cornell University, New York, New York; N. Jean Haulman, MD, David Roesel, MD, Elaine C. Jong, MD, University of Washington and Harborview Medical Center, Seattle, Washington; William M. Stauffer, MD, Patricia F. Walker, MD, University of Minnesota and HealthPartners, Minneapolis and St. Paul, Minnesota; Phyllis E. Kozarsky, MD, Henry M. Wu, MD, Jessica Fairley, MD, Carlos Franco-Paredes, MD, Emory University, Atlanta, Georgia; Christina M. Coyle, MD, MS, Murray Wittner, MD, PhD, Albert Einstein School of Medicine, Bronx, New York; Lin H. Chen, MD, Mary E. Wilson, MD, Mount Auburn Hospital,

Harvard University, Cambridge, Massachusetts; Carmelo Licitra, MD, Antonio Crespo, MD, Orlando Regional Health Center, Orlando, Florida; Noreen A. Hynes, MD, R. Bradley Sack, MD, ScD, Robin McKenzie, MD, Johns Hopkins University, Baltimore, Maryland; John D. Cahill, MD, George McKinley, MD, St. Luke's-Roosevelt Hospital Center, New York, New York; Stefan Hagmann, MD, Michael Henry, MD, Andy O. Miller, MD, Bronx-Lebanon Hospital Center, Bronx, New York; Alejandra Gurtman, MD, Mount Sinai Medical Center, New York City, New York (October 2002–August 2005); Thomas B. Nutman, MD, Amy D. Klion, MD, National Institutes of Health, Bethesda, Maryland; David O. Freedman, MD, University of Alabama at Birmingham, Alabama; Johnnie A. Yates, MD, Vernon Ansdell, MD, Kaiser Permanente, Honolulu, Hawaii; Michael W. Lynch, MD, Fresno International Travel Medical Center, Fresno, California (August 2003–February 2010); Elizabeth D. Barnett, MD, Boston University, Boston, Massachusetts; Susan Anderson, MD, Palo Alto Medical Foundation, Palo Alto, California; Susan McLellan, MD, Tulane University, New Orleans, Louisiana (December 1999–August 2005); Paul Holtom, MD, Jeffrey A. Goad, PharmD, Anne Anglim, MD, University of Southern California, Los Angeles, California (April 2007–December 2009); Nancy Piper Jenks, MS, and Christine A. Kerr, MD, Hudson River Health Care, Peekskill, New York; Abinash Virk, MD, Irene Sia, MD, Mayo Clinic, Rochester, Minnesota (October 2009–March 2010).

References

1. World Tourism Organization. UNWTO tourism highlights: 2012 edition. Madrid, Spain: World Tourism Organization; 2012. Available at http://mkt.unwto.org/en/publication/unwto-tourism-highlights-2012-edition. Accessed June 25, 2013.
2. U.S. Department of Commerce. 2009 United States resident travel abroad. Available at http://tinet.ita.doc.gov/outreachpages/download_data_table/2009_US_travel_Abroad.pdf. Accessed date TBD.
3. Institute of International Education. Open doors 2011 "fast facts." Available at http://www.iie.org/Research-and-Publications/Open-Doors/Data/Fast-Facts. Accessed June 25, 2013.
4. Office of Travel and Tourism Industries. Profile of U.S. resident travelers visiting overseas destinations: 2011 outbound. Available at http://tinet.ita.doc.gov/outreachpages/download_data_table/2011_Outbound_Profile.pdf. Accessed June 25, 2013.
5. Steffen R, Rickenbach M, Wilhelm U, Helminger A, Schar M. Health problems after travel to developing countries. J Infect Dis 1987;156:84–91.
6. Hill DR. Health problems in a large cohort of Americans traveling to developing countries. J Travel Med 2000;7:259–66.
7. Steffen R, deBernardis C, Baños A. Travel epidemiology—a global perspective. Int J Antimicrob Agents 2003;21:89–95.
8. Bacaner N, Stauffer B, Boulware DR, Walter PF, Keystone JS. Travel medicine considerations for North American immigrants visiting friends and relatives. JAMA 2004;291:2856–64.
9. Angell SY, Cetron MS. Health disparities among travelers visiting friends and relatives abroad. Ann Intern Med 2005;142:67–72.
10. CDC. Update: outbreak of severe acute respiratory syndrome—worldwide, 2003. MMWR 2003;52:241–8.
11. CDC. Update: novel influenza A (H1N1) virus infections—worldwide, May 6, 2009. MMWR 2009;58:453–8.
12. CDC. Measles—United States, 2011. MMWR 2012;61:253–7.
13. CDC. Update: mumps outbreak—New York and New Jersey, June 2009 January 2010. MMWR 2010;59:125–9.
14. CDC. Locally acquired dengue—Key West, Florida, 2009–2010. MMWR 2010;59:577–81.
15. Odolini S, Gautret P, Parola P. Epidemiology of imported malaria in the Mediterranean region. Mediterr J Hematol Infect Dis 2012;4: e2012031. Available at http://www.ncbi.nlm.nih.gov/pmc/articles/PMC3375659. Accessed June 25, 2013.
16. CDC. Malaria—Great Exuma, Bahamas, May–June 2006. MMWR 2006;55:1013–6.
17. Freedman DO, Kozarsky PE, Weld LH, Cetron MS. GeoSentinel: the global emerging infections sentinel network of the International Society of Travel Medicine. J Travel Med 1999;6:94–8.
18. Hill DR, Behrens RH. A survey of travel clinics throughout the world. J Travel Med 1996;3:46–51.
19. Leder K, Torresi J, Libman M, et al. GeoSentinel surveillance of illness in returned travelers, 2007–2011. Ann Intern Med 2013;158:456–68.
20. Freedman DO, Weld LH, Kozarsky PE, et al. Spectrum of disease and relation to place of exposure among ill returned travelers. N Engl J Med 2006;354:119–30.
21. Moore D, Edwards M, Escombe R, et al. African trypanosomiasis in travelers returning to the United Kingdom. Emerg Infect Dis 2002;8:74–6.
22. ProMED-Mail. Trypanosomiasis—US ex Zambia (eastern). Available at http://www.promedmail.org/direct.php?id=20100915.3338. Accessed June 25, 2013.
23. Cottle L, Peters J, Hall A, et al. Multiorgan dysfunction caused by travel-associated African Trypanosomiasis. Emerg Infect Dis 2012;18:287–9.
24. Simarro PP, Franco JR, Cecchi G, et al. Human African trypanosomiasis in non-endemic countries (2000–2010). J Travel Med 2012;19:44–53.
25. Florescu SA, Popescu CP, Calistru P, et al. *Plasmodium vivax* malaria in a Romanian traveler returning from Greece, August 2011. Eurosurveillance 2011;16. Available at http://www.eurosurveillance.org/ViewArticle.aspx?ArticleId=19954. Accessed June 25, 2013.
26. ProMED-Mail. Malaria vivax—Germany ex Greece. Available at http://www.promedmail.org/direct.php?id=20000713.1158. Accessed date TBD.
27. Danis K, Baka A, Lenglet A, et al. Autochthonous *Plasmodium vivax* malaria in Greece, 2011. Eurosurveillance 2011;16. Available at http://www.eurosurveillance.org/ViewArticle.aspx?ArticleId=19993. Accessed June 25, 2013.
28. ProMED-Mail. Sarcocystosis, human—Malaysia: Tioman Island. Available at http://www.promedmail.org/direct.php?id=20111031.3240. Accessed June 25, 2013.
29. CDC. Acute muscular sarcocystosis among returning travelers—Tioman Island, Malaysia, 2011. MMWR 2012;61:37–8.
30. Brunette GW, Kozarsky P, Magill AJ, Shlim DR, Whatley A, eds. CDC health information for international travel. New York, NY: Oxford University Press; 2012.
31. CDC. Update: outbreak of acute febrile illness among athletes participating in eco-challenge-Sabah 2000—Borneo, Malaysia, 2000. MMWR 2001;50:21–4.
32. Mali S, Kachur SP, Arguin PM. Malaria surveillance—United States 2010. MMWR 2012;61(No. SS-2)
33. Keystone J. Immigrants returning home to visit friends and relatives. In: Brunette GW, Kozarsky P, Magill AJ, Shlim DR, Whatley A, eds. CDC health information for international travel. New York, NY: Oxford University Press; 2012:547–51.
34. CDC. Travelers' health: see a doctor before you travel. Atlanta, GA: US Department of Health and Human Services, CDC; 2013. Available at http://www.cdc.gov/travel/page/see-doctor. Accessed June 25, 2013.
35. Leder K, Black J, O'Brien D, et al. Malaria in travelers: a review of the GeoSentinel surveillance network. Clin Infect Dis 2004; 39:1104–12.
36. Schwartz E, Weld LH, Wilder-Smith A, et al. Seasonality, annual trends, and characteristics of dengue among ill returned travelers, 1997–2006. Emerg Infect Dis 2008;14:1081–8.

Appendix A
GeoSentinel Questionnaire

Patient ID #: ABC-_____

GeoSentinel Questionnaire – SITE NAME

1. General Information	Gender □ Male □ Female	Age	*Today's Date (Clinic Visit Date):	Month/Day/Year
*Country of Birth			Primary Country of Residence Before Age 10	
*Country of Citizenship			*Country of Current Residence	
□ Immigrant	If you were not born in USA, indicate as closely as possible the date you first arrived here:			Month/Day/Year

2. History of Recent Travel	*List in order, starting with the most recent trip, all international travel in the past 6 months. Using 1 line for each separate trip, list each country visited during that trip. Indicate if the trip included travel on a Ship.*

Trip	*Trip Start Date Month/Day/Year	*Trip End Date Month/Day/Year	*Country 1	*Country 2	*Country 3	*Country 4	*Country 5
1							
2							
3							
4							
5							
6							

3. History of Previous Travel	*List all countries visited or resided in over the past 5 years (exclude country of current residence and travel in the past 6 months listed above).* **1.** <u>List each country only once.</u> **2.** CHECK the year(s) of travel to that country. **3.** CHECK the box below the year if any stay in that country in that year was longer than 30 consecutive days.

*Country:	1						2						3						4						5					
*Check each year of travel to the country	□ 2011	□ 2010	□ 2009	□ 2008	□ 2007	□ 2006	□ 2011	□ 2010	□ 2009	□ 2008	□ 2007	□ 2006	□ 2011	□ 2010	□ 2009	□ 2008	□ 2007	□ 2006	□ 2011	□ 2010	□ 2009	□ 2008	□ 2007	□ 2006	□ 2011	□ 2010	□ 2009	□ 2008	□ 2007	□ 2006
Check if stay was >30 consecutive days	□	□	□	□	□	□	□	□	□	□	□	□	□	□	□	□	□	□	□	□	□	□	□	□	□	□	□	□	□	□
*Country:	6						7						8						9						10					
*Check each year of travel to the country	□ 2011	□ 2010	□ 2009	□ 2008	□ 2007	□ 2006	□ 2011	□ 2010	□ 2009	□ 2008	□ 2007	□ 2006	□ 2011	□ 2010	□ 2009	□ 2008	□ 2007	□ 2006	□ 2011	□ 2010	□ 2009	□ 2008	□ 2007	□ 2006	□ 2011	□ 2010	□ 2009	□ 2008	□ 2007	□ 2006
Check if stay was >30 consecutive days	□	□	□	□	□	□	□	□	□	□	□	□	□	□	□	□	□	□	□	□	□	□	□	□	□	□	□	□	□	□

Version: MARCH 2012

Patient ID #: ABC-_____

GeoSentinel Questionnaire continued – SITE NAME

PATIENT SHOULD <u>NOT</u> COMPLETE THIS PAGE – TO BE COMPLETED BY CLINICIAN ONLY

Country of Exposure > 5 years ago: If a country of exposure that is related to a Final Diagnosis for the current illness was visited more than 5 years ago, add that country to the history of previous travel (section 3 on other side) and indicate that travel there occurred >5 years ago (use the notation <2006).

---

4. Exposure Details

*Country of Exposure/Other (Check the applicable boxes and/or enter up to 2 countries. *The country(s) where the current illness as defined by the final diagnosis was to a high degree of certainty acquired. A single country of exposure is the preferred standard. However, 2 countries may be designated if the likelihood of exposure is almost equal amongst the 2 countries. Exposure Country Not Ascertainable should be selected for situations where it is not possible to attribute Country of Exposure.*):

☐ Exposure Country Not Ascertainable   ☐ Ship   ☐ Plane

Country 1: _____   Country 2: _____

More Specific Place of Exposure: *(below level of country, i.e. city, state, location, event; leave blank if 2 countries are listed above)*

---

*Reason for Travel Related to Current Illness (Check One):

☐ Tourism   ☐ Business   ☐ Missionary/Volunteer/Researcher/Aid Work   ☐ Student

☐ Medical Tourism   ☐ Immigration   ☐ Visiting Friends & Relatives   ☐ Military

---

*Mark if Expatriate (Check if applicable):   ☐ Expatriate

---

*Clinical Setting (Check One):   ☐ Seen During Travel   ☐ Seen After Travel   ☐ Immigration Travel Only

---

*Patient Type (Check One):   ☐ Inpatient   ☐ Outpatient   ☐ TeleConsult-Outpatient   ☐ TeleConsult-Inpatient

---

*Did the patient have a pre-travel encounter with a health care provider? (Check One):   ☐ Yes   ☐ No   ☐ Don't Know

---

*Main Presenting Symptoms (Check at least one symptom below, but include all symptoms that apply):

☐ Abnormal Lab Test   ☐ Screening   ☐ Cardiac   ☐ Fatigue   ☐ Fever   ☐ Gastrointestinal   ☐ Genitourinary

☐ HEENT   ☐ Lymphatic   ☐ Musculoskeletal   ☐ Neurologic   ☐ Psychologic   ☐ Respiratory   ☐ Skin

☐ Other   If 'Other', Specify: _____

---

5. Diagnoses

Dx #	Working Diagnosis	Working Dx Status (circle one)	*Final Diagnosis	*Final Dx Status (circle one)
1		C P S E CT PT ST		C P S
2		C P S E CT PT ST		C P S
3		C P S E CT PT ST		C P S
4		C P S E CT PT ST		C P S
5		C P S E CT PT ST		C P S

Dx Status Legend C = Confirmed; P = Probable; S = Suspected; E = Exclusion of; CT, PT, ST = Status Post (Confirmed, Probable, Suspected)

*Is the main diagnosis causing today's visit travel related?   ☐ Travel Related   ☐ Not Ascertainable   ☐ (Not Travel Related)**
(Check the applicable box)   ***Do not enter into GeoSentinel unless needed for Site's own internal use.*

Check *Travel Related* if the main diagnosis causing today's visit is related to travel; includes Immigrants with only primary immigration travel. Check *Not Ascertainable* in situations where possible incubation periods preclude a determination of whether diagnosis was travel related or not. *(Not Travel Related)* patients are those primarily diagnosed with an infection or disease that was acquired or existed at home prior to departure or which was acquired after travel but prior to the clinic visit; Main Presenting Symptoms are still required, however all other fields in the Exposure Details section are optional, but should still be answered with reference to the reason for the clinic visit.

---

* = *These items are required fields for successful online data entry. Note: Sections 2 & 3 may be omitted if not applicable.*
Version: MARCH 2012

Appendix B
Classification of Diagnoses, by Syndrome/System Grouping — GeoSentinel Surveillance System

Acute diarrhea

Amebas, other (*Entamoeba hartmani, Escherichia nana, E. coli, E. polecki*)
Clostridium difficile–associated disease
Campylobacter
Cholera (toxigenic *Vibrio cholerae*)
Cryptosporidium
Cyclospora
Diarrhea, acute bacterial
Diarrhea, acute parasitic
Diarrhea, acute unspecified
Diarrhea, acute viral
Dientamebiasis (*Dientamoeba fragilis*)
Dysentery, acute unspecified
Entamoeba histolytica, ameboma
E. histolytica, diarrhea
E. histolytica, dysentery
E. histolytica/dispar, accompanying diarrhea
Food poisoning
Gastroenteritis
Giardia
Isospora
Noncholera *Vibrio*
Salmonella, other
Shiga toxin-producing *Escherichia coli*
Shigella, *S. boydii*
Shigella, *S. dysenteriae*
Shigella, *S. flexneri*
Shigella, *S. sonnei*
Yersinia species, nonpestis

Chronic diarrhea

Colitis, ulcerative
Crohn disease
Diarrhea, chronic responsive to antiparasitic drugs
Diarrhea, chronic unknown
Inflammatory bowel disease, new onset post-travel (Crohn or ulcerative colitis)
Irritable bowel syndrome
Irritable bowel syndrome, postinfectious
Lactose intolerance, postinfectious
Malabsorption
Sprue, tropical

Gastrointestinal, other

Abscess, pyogenic liver
Anal fissure
Anisakis
Appendicitis
Ascaris, intestinal
Biliary disease, other (includes cholelithiasis and biliary colic)
Blastocystis sp.
Celiac disease
Chilomastix mesnili
Cholangitis, nonparasitic
Cholecystitis
Clonorchis
Colitis, unspecified
Colonic polyposis
Constipation
Cyclic vomiting syndrome
Diverticulitis
Dyspepsia
E. histolytica, extraintestinal
E. histolytica/dispar, asymptomatic
Echinococcosis, hepatic
Echinococcosis, hepatic and nonhepatic
Enterobiaisis (pinworm)
Esophagitis
Fasciola
Gastritis, *Helicobacter pylori* (-)
Gastritis, *H. pylori* (+)
Gastritis, nonspecified
Gastrointestinal bleeding nonspecified
Gastrointestinal bleeding, diverticular
Gastroesophageal reflux disease
Helminth, intestinal (not diarrhea), unspecified
Hemorrhoids
Hepatic steatosis
Hepatitis A, acute
Hepatitis B carrier, asymptomatic
Hepatitis B, acute
Hepatitis B, chronic
Hepatitis C, acute
Hepatitis C, chronic
Hepatitis Delta
Hepatitis E

Hepatitis, acute unspecified
Hepatitis, chronic unspecified
Hepatomegaly
Hernia
Heterophyes heterophyes infection
Hookworm (A. duodenal, N. Americana)
Nausea, vomiting
Pain, abdominal
Pancreatitits
Peptic ulcer disease, *H. pylori* (-)
Peptic ulcer disease, *H. pylori* (+)
Peptic ulcer disease, unspecified
Perforated ulcer
Peritonitis
Protozoa, intestinal (not diarrhea), unspecified
Rectal bleeding
Schistosomiasis, *S. japonicum*
Schistosomiasis, *S. mansoni*
Schistosomiasis, *S. mekongi*
Scombroid, poisoning
Strongyloides, simple intestinal
Tapeworm, *D. latum*
Tapeworm, *H. nana*
Tapeworm, *T. saginata*
Tapeworm, *T. solium*
Tapeworm, unspecified
Trematode, other
Trichomonas intestinalis
Trichuris trichiura (whipworm)

Febrile/Systemic illness

Abscess, pyogenic (not skin, not tonsillar, not liver, not dental)
Adenitis, lymphadentis
Anaplasma phagocytophilum (human granulocytic anaplasmosis)
Babesiosis
Bacteremia
Barmah Forest Virus
Bartonella bacilliformis
Bartonella henselae (other than cat scratch disease)
Blastomycosis
Brucellosis, acute
Brucellosis, chronic
Cat scratch disease (*Bartonella henselae*)
Chagas disease, acute
Chikungunya virus infection
Coccidiomycosis
Cryptococcosis
Cytomegalovirus

Dengue (severe or complicated)
Dengue, uncomplicated
Diphtheria
Ebola virus
Ehrlichia chafeensis (human monocytic ehrlichiosos)
Endocarditis
Enterovirus 71 (EV-71)
Epstein-Barr virus
Familial Mediterranean fever
Febrile illness unspecified (<3 weeks)
Febrile illness unspecified (≥3 weeks)
Hand-foot-and-mouth disease
Hantavirus
Hemorrhagic fever syndrome, acute
Histoplasmosis
HIV, acute infection (febrile)
Lassa fever
Leptospirosis
Malaria, drug-resistant, atovaquone-resistant
Malaria, drug-resistant, chloroquine-resistant *P. falciparum*
Malaria, drug-resistant, chloroquine-resistant *P. vivax*
Malaria, drug-resistant, mefloquine-resistant
Malaria, drug-resistant, primaquine-resistant *P. vivax*
Malaria, drug-resistant, quinine-resistant *P. falciparum*
Malaria, *P. falciparum*
Malaria, *P. knowlesi*
Malaria, *P. malariae*
Malaria, *P. ovale*
Malaria, *P. vivax*
Malaria, severe and complicated, cerebral
Malaria, severe and complicated, noncerebral
Malaria, species unknown
Mastitis
Measles
Melioidosis
Meningococcal sepsis (nonmeningeal)
Mononucleosis, unspecified
Mumps
Mycobacterium tuberculosis, disseminated/miliary
Mycobacterium tuberculosis, extrapulmonary
Paracoccidioidomycosis
Parvovirus
Poliomyelitis
Pyomyositis
Q Fever (*Coxiella burnetii*)
Relapsing fever
Rickettsia akari (rickettsialpox)
Rickettsia felis
Rickettsia (now orientia) tsutsugamushi
Rickettsia prowazeki (epidemic typhus, louse borne)

Rickettsia, species unknown
Rickettsia, tick borne spotted fever (*R. africae, R. conorii,*
  R. rickettsii, and other)
Rickettsia typhi (flea-borne murine typhus)
Rift Valley fever
Roseola
Ross River virus
Rubella
Salmonella Paratyphi
Salmonella Typhi
Sepsis
Smallpox (*Variola major*)
Streptococcal toxin disease (scarlet fever)
Toxoplasma gondii
Trypanosomiasis, African (*T.B. gambiense*)
Trypanosomiasis, African (*T.B. rhodesiense*)
Tularemia
Typhoid fever (enteric fever), unspecified
Varicella (chickenpox)
Viral syndrome (no rash)
Viral syndrome with rash
Yellow fever
Yersinia pestis, bubonic

Respiratory
Acute respiratory distress syndrome (ARDS)
Allergic rhinitis
Anthrax, pulmonary
Asthma
Bronchitis, acute
Bronchitis, chronic
Bronchospasm
Eosinophilia, tropical pulmonary
Eustachian tube dysfunction (ETD)
Hemoptysis
High altitude pulmonary edema
Influenza-like illness
Influenza A
Influenza B
Influenza, avian
Influenza, novel H1N1 (swine)
Legionnaires' disease
Mycobacterium tuberculosis (multidrug resistant or extreme
  drug resistant)
Mycobacterium tuberculosis, pulmonary
Mycobacterium, atypical, in the lung
Otitis (serious)
Otitis externa
Otitis media, acute
Perforation, tympanic membrane

Pertussis
Pertussis
Pleural effusion
Pleurisy
Pneumonia, atypical (diffuse)
Pneumonia, bacterial (lobar)
Pneumonia, fungal
Respiratory tract infection (upper)
Sever acute respiratory syndrome (SARS)
Sinusitis, acute
Sinusitis, chronic
Yersinia pestis, pneumonic

Dermatologic
Anthrax, cutaneous
Bite, animal other
Bite, cat
Bite, dog
Bite, human
Bite, insect (includes sting)
Bite, insect superinfected
Bite, monkey
Bite, scorpion
Bite, spider
Bite, tick
Burn
Cercarial dermatitis (human)
Creeping eruption other than hookworm-related CLM
Cutaneous larva migrans (CLM), hookworm-related
Cyst
Erythema chronicum migrans
Erythema multiforme
Erythema nodosum
Frostbite
Fungal infection (superficial/cutaneous mycosis)
Fungal infection, subcutaneous
Gnathostoma
Herpes zoster, shingles
Leishmania, cutaneous
Leishmania, mycocutaneous
Leprosy
Lice
Lymphangitis
Marine envenomation
Mites
Mycobacterium, atypical (cutaneous)
Myiasis
Neurodermatitis
Pilonidal cyst
Pruritis, unknown origin

Psoriasis
Rabies, postexposure prophylaxis
Rash, atopic dermatitis
Rash, contact dermatitis
Rash, drug-related
Rash, heat-induced
Rash, petechial
Rash, photosensitivity
Rash, sea bathers eruption
Rash, unknown etiology (non-febrile)
Rash, urticarial (angioedema)
Scabies
Scratch, monkey
Skin and soft tissue infection
Skin and soft tissue infection, secondary bacterial of existing
  lesion
Skin and soft tissue infection, superficial
Skin abscess
Solar dermatoses (chronic)
Sporotrichosis
Tumor, benign superficial
Tungiasis
Warts, nongenital
Yaws

Adverse events to medication or vaccination
Drug adverse reaction, nonmefloquine (not cutaneous)
Mefloquine intolerance, neuropsychiatric, mild
Mefloquine intolerance, neuropsychiatric, severe
Mefloquine intolerance, other (nonpsychiatric)
Vaccine adverse event (not rash)
Miscellaneous tissue parasites
Ascaris, extraintestinal
Chagas disease, chronic
Cysticercosis (muscular, cutaneous)
Echinococcosis, nonhepatic
Filaria, bancrofti
Filaria, loa loa
Filaria, onchocerciasis
Filaria, other
Filaria, species unknown
Leishmania, visceral
Schistosomiasis, human species unknown
Strongyloides, hyperinfection syndrome
Trichinella
Visceral larva migrans

Oral and dental
Dental abscess
Dental caries
Dental, other

Epistaxis
Gingivitis
Glossitis
Laryngitis
Peritonsillar abscess
Pharyngitis, nonstreptococcal
Paryngitis, streptococcal
Pharyngitis, unspecified
Stomatitis
Thrush
Tonsilitis

Ophthalmologic
Chlamydia trachomatis (ocular)
Conjunctivitis
Corneal ulcer
Eye disease, chronic
Poor vision
Sty/hordeolum/blepharitis
Visual loss

Obstetric/Gynecologic
Cervicitis
Endometritis
Menstrual disorder
Miscarriage
Ovarian cyst
Pelvic inflammatory disease/acute
Pelvic inflammatory disease/chronic
Pregnancy
Prolapse, uterine
Vaginitis

Nonspecific symptoms or findings
Alopecia (hair loss)
Anaphylaxis
Anemia
Antibiotic-resistant bacteria
Chemical intoxication
Dehydration
Edema
Eosinophilia
Failure to thrive (all ages)
Fatigue <1 month (not febrile)
Fatigue ≥1 month (not febrile)
Leukopenia
Lymphadenopathy
Lymphedema
Metabolic disorder
Micronutrient deficiency
Pain, chest (noncardiac)
Palpitations

Protein-calorie malnutrition
Sickle cell crisis
Splenomegaly
Syncope
Vitamin D deficiency/insufficiency
Weight loss
White blood cell, platelet disorder

Psychologic

Anxiety disorder, generalized
Anxiety disorder, health-related
Bipolar affective disorder
Child/adolescent behavioral disorder
Childhood developmental disorder
Delusional parasitosis
Depression – Major depressive disorder
Depression, not otherwise specified
Eating disorder
Insomnia
Jet lag
Obsessive compulsive disorder
Panic attacks/panic disorder
Psychosis
Stress, marital family
Stress, not otherwise specified
Stress, post-traumatic stress disorder
Stress, work-related
Substance abuse (includes alcohol)
Suicide attempt
Violence exposure

Neurologic

Acute mountain sickness (AMS)
Angiostrongyliasis
Ataxia
Botulism
Cerebrovascular accident (CVA)
Ciguatera intoxication
Cranial neuropathy
Dizziness
Encephalitis, acute
Encephalitis, acute, no proven viral etiology
Encephalitis, chronic
Encephalitis, Japanese
Encephalitis, Murray Valley
Encephalitis, tick borne
Encephalitis, viral
Encephalopathy, unspecified
Guillain-Barré
Headache

Hearing loss
High-altitude cerebral edema
HTLV-1/HTLV-2
Lyme disease, chronic (e.g., neurologic)
Meniere's disease
Meningitis, bacterial other
Meningitis, Eosinophilic
Meningitis, free-living amoeba
Meningitis, fungal
Meningitis, H. flu
Meningitis, meningococcal
Meningitis, pneumococcal
Meningitis, viral
Mycobacterium tuberculosis, CNS tuberculoma
Mycobacterium tuberculosis, meningitis
Neurocysticercosis
Neuropathy, peripheral
Papilledema
Poisoning, neurotoxic shellfish
Poisoning, paralytic shellfish
Polyneuritis of unknown origin
Rabies
Seizure disorder
Tetanus
Tinnitus
Transient ischemic attack (TIA)
Trigeminal neuralgia
Vertigo
West Nile virus

Genitourinary and sexually transmitted disease

Balanitis, phimosis
Chancroid
Chlamydia trachomatis (genital)
Chlamydia, lymphogranuloma venereum
Cystitis (noninfectious)
Enuresis
Genital ulcer
Gonorrhea
Hematuria
Hemolytic uremic syndrome (Shiga toxin-associated)
Herpes simplex
Kidney stone/urine stone
Prostatitis, acute
Prostatitis, chronic
Proteinuria
Pyelonephitis
Renal failure, acute
Renal failure, chronic
Schistosomiasis, *Schistosoma haematobium*

Sexually transmitted disease
Syphilis
Trichomonas vaginalis
Urethritis, gonococcal
Urethritis, nongonococcal
Urethritis, unspecified
Urinary retention
Urinary tract infection, acute
Warts, genital

Injury and musculoskeletal
Abrasion
Arthralgia
Arthritis, nonseptic
Arthritis, septic
Bursitis
Carpal tunnel syndrome
Contusion
Fibromyalgia
Foreign body
Fracture
Head injury
Hematoma
Ingrown toenail
Joint dislocation
Laceration
Lyme disease, arthritis
Multiple sclerosis
Myalgia
Pain, back
Pain, knee
Pain, leg
Pain, neck
Pain, shoulder
Plantar fasciitis
Sciatica
Sprain/strain
Tendinitis
Trauma or injury, miscellaneous

Chronic disease
AIDS
Autoimmune disorders
Cancer
Cancer, hematologic
Cerebral palsy
Chronic obstructive pulmonary disease (COPD)
Cirrhosis
Diabetes
G6PD deficient
HIV-asymptomatic
HIV, asymptomatic, newly diagnosed
Intoxication, lead
Parkinson's disease
Reiter's syndrome
Scoliosis
Thalassemia
Thyroid disease
Tuberculosis, positive PPD or positive quantiferon or positive t-spot (not active disease)

Cardiovascular
Congestive heart failure (CHF)
Heart disease, arrythmia
Heart disease, coronary artery disease, angina
Heart disease, other
Hypertension
Myocarditis
Pericarditis
Pulmonary embolism
Thombophelebitis